The Mystery of the Golden Feather

For Eugene and Lily

The Mystery of the Golden Feather

Tessa Strickland

Illustrated by
Clara Anganuzzi

DK

WELCOME

As you begin this story, I invite you to pause, close your eyes, and listen. What can you hear? Perhaps the sound of cars, or the voices of people talking, or even the whirr of a washing machine. Perhaps, if you settle down for a while and let your mind be quiet, you can also hear a snatch of birdsong.

Most of the time, we don't pay attention to the natural sounds around us. The tasks of the day come rushing in, and we forget how to connect to our wild companions on this earth. But when you take some time to sit and listen, you may come to learn more about the animals around you. And you may find a little bit of peace and calm in your busy day as well.

This story is my invitation to you to slow down and let yourself find peace in nature. After the story, there are some mindfulness exercises that you can practice. When you are mindful, the world inside you and the world outside you come together. By listening out for birds, you wake up your other senses, too. You feel more alive, alert, and peaceful at the same time. As you tune in, you may also feel a new sense of belonging.

The best time of year to listen to birds is in the spring. And the best time of day is in the morning. You can hear birds all year round, though. And just as you notice the birds in your neighborhood, they will notice you. Before long, you'll learn to recognize them not just by their melodies but also by their feathers and their colors, just like the boy in this story.

Tessa Strickland

Early one morning,
Felix found a *feather*
on his windowsill.

It was a beautiful *feather,*
unlike anything he had ever seen
in his entire life.

He drew a picture to remember the lovely sight.

He showed it to his mom.

"Isn't that exquisite!" she said.

"I wonder what bird it comes from."

At circle time, Felix showed the *feather* sketch to his class.

"Pass it around!" shouted Lyra.

"Let me have a closer look!"

10

"I wonder what bird this *feather* comes from," said the teacher.

"I bet it's an eagle," said Frank.

"Parrot, parrot, parrot!" chanted Annabel.

"Maybe it's from a phoenix!" said Connor, "Or even a peacock."

11

Felix was not convinced.
He went to the community garden
to find Ralph.

Ralph was the wisest person Felix knew.
And Ralph knew stuff about birds.

"That's a very fine *feather*, Felix," said Ralph.

"Where did you find it?"

"It was lying on my windowsill," said Felix.

"Oh really? Then we'd better find
out who put it there."

"How do we do that?"

"Well now," said Ralph, "we'd better ask the birds.
But first, we'll need to **listen** for a little while."

Ralph and Felix sat very
quietly on the bench in the garden.
They listened intently.

"There are so **many** songs!" said Felix.
"How do I know which is which?"

"Well now," said Ralph, "do you hear that tune?"

"The one that sounds a bit like a flute?"

"That's the one. This *feather* here can't come from him—he's an **American Robin**."

"What about the bird singing

dzi dzi dzi dzi dzi dzeer?"

"That'll be an Eastern Kingbird," said Ralph.
"They've just flown in from South America.
But I don't think your *feather* comes from one of them."

Ralph and Felix sat still for a long time. The more they sat, the more birds Felix could hear.

"What about the really noisy one? The one with a trill at the end?"

"Ah yes," said Ralph. "That's a **House Wren**. It's got a big voice for such a tiny bird. See, it's over there, screaming at the **Blue Jay**."

Felix got fidgety. "How does this work?"
he asked. "How do we know what bird
it is just by listening?"

"Shhhh," said Ralph. "Hear that?"

"What?" whispered Felix.
"High up or low down?"

Ralph gave him a knowing look.
"Low down, son. Low down."

Tweet... tweet... tweet-tweet-tweet... tmr.

"Got it?"

Felix nodded. "It's so bright—like a smile."

"When you go to bed tonight, ask the bird who makes that sound to show itself."

"How do I do that?"

Ralph shrugged and started to
separate his seedlings.

That night,
Felix turned the
birdsong around
and around
in his mind.

In his dreams, he saw
all kinds of beautiful birds,
but he couldn't tell
which was his.

The next morning, Felix went back to the garden. There was no sign of Ralph, so he sat by himself and listened. He could hear his heart beating...

and he could hear lots of birds.

"This is impossible,"
thought Felix.

Then he heard the song he was waiting for.

Tweet... tweet... tweet-tweet-tweet... trrr.

He followed the sound with his eyes—and there they were,
a whole group of birds, beside Ralph's rickety shed.

Ralph appeared. "Open your hands," he whispered.
"Now, keep very still and wait."

Felix waited…

and waited...

and waited.

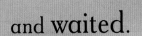

And then, one, two,

three **American Goldfinches** flew up...

and ate out of his hand.

35

THE MAGIC OF MINDFULNESS

As Felix uncovers the mystery of the golden feather, he is also learning to practice mindfulness. Mindfulness is a simple, practical tool that can help children become aware of themselves and connect with the world around them. These pages introduce some mindfulness exercises you can share and enjoy with your child.

FIND A QUIET PLACE

You can practice mindfulness at home. Or maybe create an opportunity to enjoy nature. Go for a walk, or find a local green space where you will be able to take a quiet moment. Perhaps you can listen to the birds singing, observe small animals, or simply notice your own thoughts.

BE STILL

Nature is all around us. Birds, insects, squirrels; the sun, the wind, petals floating on the breeze. When you're sitting still and quiet, animals may well come out of their hiding spots. With practice, your child will see that being peaceful can be rewarding.

EXPAND AWARENESS

Encourage your child to focus on something they see or a sound they hear—perhaps a slow-moving cloud, or the rumble of traffic. Once they have picked something, guide them to slowly let their eyes and ears notice more and more.

SET AN INTENTION

When Felix asks the mystery bird to show itself in his dream, this is an aspect of mindfulness known as "setting an intention." When you need to focus on a goal, it helps to picture in your mind what you wish for.

BREATHE

Often, we are so busy thinking or worrying that we don't notice the little things around us. Encourage your child to focus on their body and their breathing. Breathe slowly and quietly. Suggest breathing in for a count of four, then out for a count of six a few times.

BE PATIENT

Let your child know that it's okay if nothing is happening right now. Let them feel the fresh air on their face.

Guide them to realize there is always something to appreciate in nature.

BE PRESENT

Enjoy just being part of nature—part of this ever-changing, always moving, alive, and wonderful world.

MEET THE AUTHOR

Tessa grew up in rural Yorkshire, England in a very cold house with a big vegetable garden and lots of birds. She started writing when she was in elementary school and still likes nothing better than dreaming up stories and getting them onto the page. She also works as a mindfulness-based psychotherapist.

MEET THE ILLUSTRATOR

Clara grew up in Seychelles, where she would draw on every surface she could find. She has always had a love of nature and all types of critters, who often inhabit her drawings. Clara now spends her days in Bristol, England doodling in her plant-filled studio overlooking the city.

Penguin
Random
House

Written by Tessa Strickland
Illustrated by Clara Anganuzzi
Subject Consultants Joseph DiCostanzo, Wynne Kinder
US Senior Editor Shannon Beatty
Project Editors Shari Last, Robin Moul
Project Art Editor Polly Appleton
Designers Veneta Cooper, Holly Price
Managing Editor Penny Smith
Deputy Art Director Mabel Chan
Senior Production Editor Nikoleta Parasaki
Production Controller Magdalena Bojko
Jacket Designer Polly Appleton
Jacket Coordinator Magda Pszuk
Publisher Francesca Young
Publishing Director Sarah Larter
Thanks to William Collins, Tom Morse

First American Edition, 2023
Published in the United States by DK Publishing
1745 Broadway, 20th Floor, New York, NY 10019

Text copyright © Tessa Strickland 2023
Layout and design © 2023 Dorling Kindersley Limited
DK, a Division of Penguin Random House LLC
23 24 25 26 27 10 9 8 7 6 5 4 3 2 1
001-332252-May/2023

A catalog record for this book
is available from the Library of Congress.
ISBN: 978-0-7440-6989-1

DK books are available at special discounts when purchased in bulk for sales promotions, premiums, fund-raising, or educational use. For details, contact: DK Publishing Special Markets, 1745 Broadway, 20th Floor, New York, NY 10019
SpecialSales@dk.com

Printed and bound in China

For the curious
www.dk.com

This book was made with Forest Stewardship Council™ certified paper – one small step in DK's commitment to a sustainable future.
For more information go to
www.dk.com/our-green-pledge

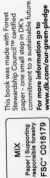